The European Union

Political, Social, and Economic Cooperation

THE EUROPEAN UNION

POLITICAL, SOCIAL, AND ECONOMIC COOPERATION

Austria

Belgium

Cyprus

Czech Republic

Denmark

Estonia

The European Union: Facts and Figures

Finland

France

Germany

Greece

Hungary

Ireland

Italy

Latvia

Lithuania

Luxembourg

Malta

The Netherlands

Poland

Portugal

Slovakia

Slovenia

Spain

Sweden

United Kingdom

The European Union

Political, Social, and Economic Cooperation

PORTUGAL

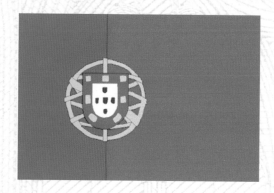

by
Kim Etingoff

Mason Crest Publishers
Philadelphia

Mason Crest Publishers Inc.
370 Reed Road, Broomall, Pennsylvania 19008
(866) MCP-BOOK (toll free)
www.masoncrest.com

First printing
1 2 3 4 5 6 7 8 9 10

Library of Congress Cataloging-in-Publication Data

Etingoff, Kim.
    Portugal / by Kim Etingoff.
        p. cm.—(The European Union: political, social, and economic cooperation)
    Includes index.
        ISBN 1-4222-0059-0
        ISBN 1-4222-0038-8 (series)
1. Portugal—Juvenile literature. 2. European Union—Portugal—Juvenile literature. I. Title. II. European Union (Series) (Philadelphia, Pa.)
    DP517.E84 2006
    946.9—dc22
                                            2005020107

Produced by Harding House Publishing Service, Inc.
www.hardinghousepages.com
Interior design by Benjamin Stewart.
Cover design by MK Bassett-Harvey.
Printed in the Hashemite Kingdom of Jordan.

CONTENTS

INTRODUCTION 8

1. THE LANDSCAPE 11

2. PORTUGAL'S HISTORY AND GOVERNMENT 19

3. THE ECONOMY 33

4. PORTUGAL'S PEOPLE AND CULTURE 39

5. THE CITIES 47

6. THE FORMATION OF THE EUROPEAN UNION 53

7. PORTUGAL IN THE EUROPEAN UNION 67

A CALENDAR OF PORTUGUESE FESTIVALS 74

RECIPES 75

PROJECT AND REPORT IDEAS 79

CHRONOLOGY 81

FURTHER READING/INTERNET RESOURCES 82

FOR MORE INFORMATION 83

GLOSSARY 84

INDEX 86

PICTURE CREDITS 87

BIOGRAPHIES 88

THE EUROPEAN UNION

BARENTS SEA

GREENLAND SEA

★ Reykjavik · ICELAND

NORWEGIAN SEA

White Sea

· Trondheim

FINLAND

· Tampere
· Turku · Helsinki ✪

NORWAY
· Bergen · Lillehammer
Oslo ✪
· Kristiansand

SWEDEN
Stockholm ✪
· Norrköping

Gulf of Bothnia

Gulf of Finland ★ Tallin

ESTONIA
· Tartu

Gulf of Riga
· Ventspils
· Liepaja · Riga ✪
· Daugavpils

LATVIA

★ Moscow

RUSSIA

DENMARK
· Aalborg
· Helsingborg
· Malmö
· Odense · Copenhagen ✪

· Klaipeda
· Kaunas
LITHUANIA
Vilnius ✪

RUSSIA

★ Minsk

BELARUS

UNITED KINGDOM
· Glasgow · Edinburgh
· Belfast

IRELAND
Irish Sea
· Dublin
· Killarney · Cork
· Liverpool · Manchester

NORTH SEA

BALTIC SEA

· Gdansk

POLAND
Warsaw ✪
· Wroclaw

★ Kyiv

UKRAINE

· Birmingham

THE NETHERLANDS
The Hague ·
· Rotterdam · Amsterdam
· Hamburg

· Berlin ✪
· Leipzig
· Dresden

· Krakow
· Kosice

MOLDOVA

St. George's Channel

· London
English Channel

BELGIUM
· Brussels
LUXEMBOURG
· Luxembourg

· Düsseldorf
· Cologne
GERMANY
· Frankfurt/Main
· Stuttgart

· Plzen · Prague
· Brno
CZECH REPUBLIC
· Linz
· Salzburg
SLOVAKIA
· Bratislava

★ Chisinau

FRANCE
· Paris

· Munich

AUSTRIA
· Vienna
· Györ · Budapest ✪

HUNGARY
· Szeged

ROMANIA
★ Bucharest

Sea of Azov

· Nantes

Bay of Biscay
· Bordeaux
· Lyons

SWITZERLAND
· Bern
· Geneva

· Milan
· Venice · Trieste
· Ljubljana

SLOVENIA
· Turin

CROATIA
BOSNIA-HERCEGOVINA
· Sarajevo
· Belgrade

YUGOSLAVIA

★ Sofia

BULGARIA

BLACK SEA

· Toulouse
· Bilbao

Gulf du Lion
· Marseille
· Nice

· Florence

ITALY

ADRIATIC SEA

MACEDONIA
· Skopje
· Thessaloniki

ALBANIA
· Tirana

· Ankara

TURKEY

· Vigo
· Porto

PORTUGAL
· Lisbon

· Madrid
· Barcelona

· Rome
· Naples

TYRRHENIAN SEA

AEGEAN SEA

GREECE
· Athens

SPAIN
· Valencia
· Seville
· Faro

MEDITERRANEAN SEA

Strait of Gibraltar

★ Algiers

IONIAN SEA

· Kalamata

Sea of Crete

· Lefkosia (Nicosia)
CYPRUS
· Lemesos

SYRIA

★ Rabat

MOROCCO

ALGERIA

· Tunis

MALTA
· Valetta

MEDITERRANEAN SEA

LEBANON
· Damascus

JORDAN

ISRAEL & THE PALESTINIAN TERRITORIES

TUNISIA

· Tripoli

· Cairo

LIBYA

EGYPT

PORTUGAL

European Union Member since 1986

Chaves

Braga

Vila do Conde

Vila Real

Porto

Aveiro

Viseu

Guarda

Coimbra

Figueira da Foz

Castelo
Branco

Portalegre

Santarém

Lisbon

Almada

Setúbal

Evora

Beja

Portiãmo

Faro Olhão

INTRODUCTION

Sixty years ago, Europe lay scarred from the battles of the Second World War. During the next several years, a plan began to take shape that would unite the countries of the European continent so that future wars would be inconceivable. On May 9, 1950, French Foreign Minister Robert Schuman issued a declaration calling on France, Germany, and other European countries to pool together their coal and steel production as "the first concrete foundation of a European federation." "Europe Day" is celebrated each year on May 9 to commemorate the beginning of the European Union (EU).

The EU consists of twenty-five countries, spanning the continent from Ireland in the west to the border of Russia in the east. Eight of the ten most recently admitted EU member states are former communist regimes that were behind the Iron Curtain for most of the latter half of the twentieth century.

Any European country with a democratic government, a functioning market economy, respect for fundamental rights, and a government capable of implementing EU laws and policies may apply for membership. Bulgaria and Romania are set to join the EU in 2007. Croatia and Turkey have also embarked on the road to EU membership.

While the EU began as an idea to ensure peace in Europe through interconnected economies, it has evolved into so much more today:

- Citizens can travel freely throughout most of the EU without carrying a passport and without stopping for border checks.

- EU citizens can live, work, study, and retire in another EU country if they wish.

- The euro, the single currency accepted throughout twelve of the EU countries (with more to come), is one of the EU's most tangible achievements, facilitating commerce and making possible a single financial market that benefits both individuals and businesses.

- The EU ensures cooperation in the fight against cross-border crime and terrorism.

- The EU is spearheading world efforts to preserve the environment.

- As the world's largest trading bloc, the EU uses its influence to promote fair rules for world trade, ensuring that globalization also benefits the poorest countries.

- The EU is already the world's largest donor of humanitarian aid and development assistance, providing 55 percent of global official development assistance to developing countries in 2004.

The EU is neither a nation intended to replace existing nations, nor an international organization. The EU is unique—its member countries have established common institutions to which they delegate some of their sovereignty so that decisions on matters of joint interest can be made democratically at the European level.

Europe is a continent with many different traditions and languages, but with shared values such as democracy, freedom, and social justice, cherished values well known to North Americans. Indeed, the EU motto is "United in Diversity."

Enjoy your reading. Take advantage of this chance to learn more about Europe and the EU!

Ambassador John Bruton,
Head of Delegation of the European Commission, Washington, D.C.

Fishing from the cliffs of Guincho

THE LANDSCAPE

In recent years, Portugal is often overshadowed by its larger neighbor, Spain. However, it was once a wealthy and powerful nation, owning an empire that stretched across the globe. Although it has lost much of that glory, it remains a colorful and fascinating country in modern times.

The terraced land of the Douro Valley

The smaller of the only two countries to occupy the Iberian Peninsula (the other being Spain), Portugal has an area of 2,147 square miles (92,391 square kilometers), which makes it slightly smaller than the state of Indiana. The nation also includes two Atlantic island chains: the Azores and Madeira Islands.

NORTH, CENTER, AND SOUTH: DIFFERENT LANDS

Although it only measures 350 miles (560 kilometers) from north to south, Portugal is divided geographically between these areas. The central region of the country contains its capital, Lisbon.

Geographically, this area has pine forests and gently rolling land. In the north, the land tends to be more fertile and better suited for growing crops such as corn and grapes. This region also contains several rivers and forests. For these reasons, the north is much more populated than the south. Many of its cities are located on the rivers, which provide water and trade routes, both historically and today.

The mountains of the north can be impressive; the highest peak in continental Portugal, Torre, is 6,540 feet (1,993 meters) tall. This mountain is part of the Serra da Estrela range, the highest in the country.

In the south, in the area known as the Alentejo, the land is more arid and is unable to grow as many crops, though olives, oranges, and figs are able to survive. The land is mostly made up of hills and plains. Even farther south is the Algarve, which is the driest and hottest part of Portugal.

THE ISLANDS

In the early fifteenth centuries, two island chains, or **archipelagos**, were discovered by Portugal and incorporated into the country. The Azores and Madeira islands are both located in the northern Atlantic Ocean and are inhabited by people from the mainland of Portugal, along with others from various European countries.

The Azores consist of nine islands that are peopled, as well as several islands that are uninhabited. They are located 800 miles (289 kilometers) to the west of mainland Portugal. The islands are generally forested, except for the beaches that form their coasts. The Madeira Islands, which are farther from the Iberian Peninsula, are closer to Africa than Portugal. The islands' coasts are rockier than those on the Azores, but their interiors are just as green and lush.

Volcanoes formed most of the islands. Volcanic activity helped to create the 370-mile (600-kilometer) stretch of Azorean Islands. Many of the islands are home to tall mountains, such as the volcano on Pico Island, the highest peak in all Portugal.

COASTS AND RIVERS

Much of Portuguese life centers around the 1,115-mile (1,793-kilometer) coastline. Historically, this easy access to the sea fueled Portugal's expansion and exploration.

Ten major rivers flow through Portugal. Since it provides a trade route to and from Spain and Portugal, one of the most important in the north is the Rio Duoro. The Rio Tejo, the longest river in the country, winds its way through Lisbon. Since it is deep enough to provide passage for large cargo ships, it is considered the most important commercial river in the nation.

A Temperate Climate

Portugal's climate can vary from region to region, but in general, it tends to be **temperate**. In the south, summers can become extremely hot, especially in the southern region of Algarve, but the region usually remains comfortably warm throughout the rest of the year; the average summer temperature is 78°F (25°C). The north experiences slightly cooler weather and has a distinct winter season, characterized by rain and colder temperatures. Portugal's average winter temperature is about 61°F (16°C). In the higher mountains, snowfall is not uncommon.

The coastal regions tend to be cooler since the ocean moderates the weather. The Azores, surrounded by the sea, have moderate temperatures that change little throughout the year, ranging from 55°F (13°C) to 76°F (25°C). The Madeira Islands have similar temperatures.

Flora and Fauna

Much of Portugal is covered with forests. More varieties of trees are found in the north, including pine, elm, poplar, and oak. Cork oak is the most common type of tree growing in the south. Other plants besides trees grow in Portugal, including orchids, lavender, rosemary, and broom.

The animals of Portugal are generally typical to the rest of the Iberian Peninsula. Deer, wild goats, hares, rabbits, and several types of birds are common sights. Wolves, foxes, and lynx make the mountains their homes. Portugal is also home to a number of animals that are considered endan-

---

Quick Facts: The Geography of Portugal

Location: Southwestern Europe, bordering the North Atlantic Ocean, west of Spain

Area:* slightly smaller than Indiana
  total: 35,672 square miles (92,391 sq. km.)
  land: 35,503 square miles (91,951 sq. km.)
  water: 170 miles (440 sq. km.)

Borders: Spain 754 miles (1,214 km.)

Climate: maritime temperate; cool and rainy in the north; warmer and drier in the south

Terrain: mountainous north of the Tagus River, rolling plains in the south

Elevation extremes:
  lowest point: Atlantic Ocean—0 feet (0 meters)
  highest point: Ponta de Pico (in the Azores)—7,713 feet (2,351 meters)

Natural hazards: severe earthquakes in the Azores

*Includes the Azores and Madeira Islands.
Source: www.cia.gov, 2005.

Portugal's farmland

gered. These include the fin whale, the monk seal, the Iberian lynx, the Mediterranean monk seal, and the northern right whale.

ENVIRONMENTAL CONCERNS

Like most countries, Portugal must balance its prosperity and growth with the need to protect and preserve the environment. As its population has grown, people have pushed into wild areas, destroying habitats in order to use them for farming, housing, or other human needs. In 2001, the construction of an artificial lake on the Guadiana River was finished. Many people opposed the project because of the invasive construction that was necessary.

Deforestation is also a problem. Old-growth forests, or woods that have never been cut down, are becoming rare and only exist in the more remote parts of the mountains. Portugal has set aside parts of the country for the conservation of these forests, as well as other rare habitats and wildlife. These areas are divided into a national park, twelve natural parks, and several natural reserves, natural monuments, and protected landscapes.

Some problems dealing with the environment are beyond the people of Portugal's control. In 2003, the country was victim to a series of forest fires that burned a massive area of land, killed eighteen people, and cost around a billion euros.

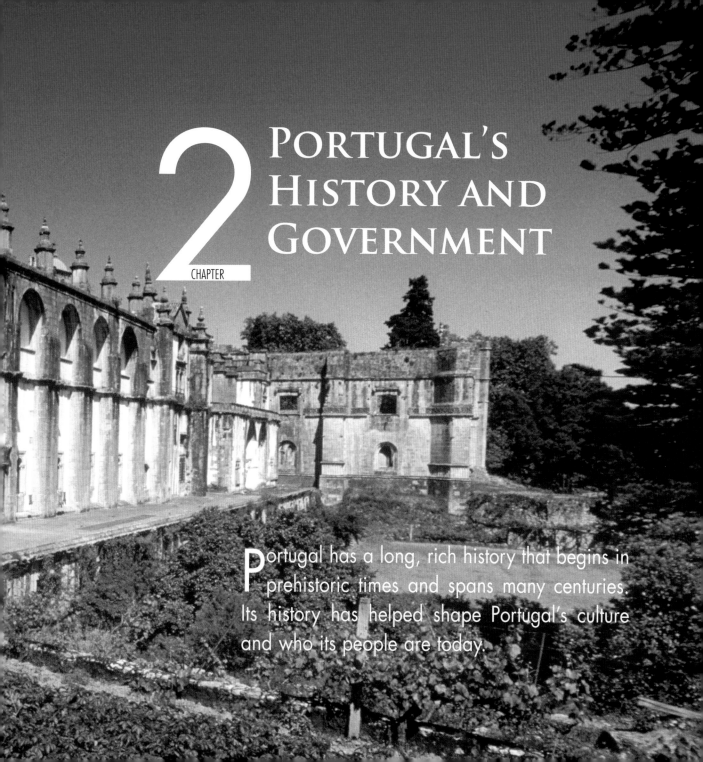

2
CHAPTER

PORTUGAL'S HISTORY AND GOVERNMENT

Portugal has a long, rich history that begins in prehistoric times and spans many centuries. Its history has helped shape Portugal's culture and who its people are today.

EARLY PORTUGAL

Scientists have speculated that people have inhabited Portugal for the past 500,000 years. **Hunter-gatherers**, who lived along river valleys, were the main residents for much of the earliest part of this time. Advanced settlements—fortified villages in the Tagus Valley—have been discovered that date back to 5500 BCE.

In 700 BCE, the peninsula was settled by a group of people known as the Celts, who arrived from Central Europe. They **assimilated** into the local culture of the people already living in the area, forming the Celt-Iberians, or Lusitanians. Many other groups followed, including the Phoenicians, Greeks, and Romans, who first invaded the peninsula in 219 BCE. The Visigoths, a Germanic tribe, conquered almost all the peninsula in the fifth century CE. These invaders came from the area around what is now Germany.

THE GOLDEN AGE OF THE MOORS AND CHRISTIAN RECONQUEST

The Moors, a group of Arabic peoples, were one of the most important influences on the Iberian Peninsula. Arriving from northern Africa, they began their occupation of present-day Portugal and Spain in 711 CE. They conquered most of the peninsula, except for one small piece of land in the northwest.

The Moors left a lasting mark on Portugal that is still evident today, especially in the Algarve in the south, which the Moors preferred to the rest of the country because of its hot, dry conditions that reminded them of their homelands. Their centuries-long inhabitance of the area, referred to as al-Andalus by the Moors, meant that the cultures of the Moors and the local Portuguese natives mixed together, forming a unique blend of customs, architecture, food, and language that can only be found on the Iberian Peninsula.

Under the Moors, peace and prosperity were brought to Portugal. Most of the natives were easily converted to Islam, although religious toleration

DATING SYSTEMS AND THEIR MEANING

You might be accustomed to seeing dates expressed with the abbreviations BC or AD, as in the year 1000 BC or the year AD 1900. For centuries, this dating system has been the most common in the Western world. However, since BC and AD are based on Christianity (BC stands for Before Christ and AD stands for *anno Domini*, Latin for "in the year of our Lord"), many people now prefer to use abbreviations that people from all religions can be comfortable using. The abbreviations BCE (meaning Before Common Era) and CE (meaning Common Era) mark time in the same way (for example, 1000 BC is the same year as 1000 BCE, and AD 1900 is the same year as 1900 CE), but BCE and CE do not have the same religious overtones as BC and AD.

An aqueduct testifies to the Romans' presence in Portugal

The Castle of Ourem

European Union—Portugal

was practiced. Education, the arts, and industry all leaped ahead, transforming Portugal into a center of culture and trade.

The occupation of the Moors ended in the eleventh century. Power-hungry Moorish nobles divided the empire between themselves, providing an opportunity for Visigothic Christians who had remained unconquered to retake the peninsula. Slowly, Christian nobles were able to regain control over the Moors, although fighting was ongoing for over two hundred years.

THE FORMATION OF PORTUGAL

The king of Astúrias-León, who had gained power after fighting the Moors, appointed nobles to rule the province of Portucalense. Soon, rule over this area became a **hereditary** title. One count, Afonso Henriques, proclaimed himself king of Portugal and was eventually recognized by the king of Astúrias-León in 1143.

Afonso Henriques and his heirs conquered the remaining Muslims, and over the period of about a century, they expanded the borders of the kingdom to form what is now the familiar shape of Portugal.

EXPANSION

In the fifteenth century, Portugal began to explore the oceans and beyond, ushering in a period of glory. The need for new trade routes, as well as the fact that the country had expanded as far as it could on the Iberian Peninsula, meant that Portugal had to look to the seas. Portugal also had advanced nautical knowledge and a good position for naval exploration.

The major force behind Portugal's exploration was Prince Henry the Navigator, the son of King João (John). Under his direction and financial help, the ships of Portugal were able to create new trade routes and a new empire. At its greatest extent, the empire reached India, Brazil, and Africa.

During the 1400s, Portugal was one of the most powerful countries in the world. The monarchy became the richest in Europe, and they established the country as a center for trade.

THE INQUISITION

Despite the prosperity that Portugal seemed to have, many problems lurked beneath the surface. Social inequality continued, and freedom of speech was not encouraged. One of the most famous examples of this is the Inquisition. This repression of freedom of religion took place in Portugal, as well as in Spain.

In 1539, the king of Portugal, João III, set up a Court of Inquisition, which tried and condemned 1,400 people to death for **heresy**. Many of those sentenced to death were Jews who had already converted to Christianity, but who were suspected of still practicing Judaism.

THE DECLINE OF PORTUGAL

The empire's wealth and power depended on the strength of the monarch. After the death of João

Braganca Palace

Tiles in Viseu portray Portuguese life in earlier centuries.

III, who had been a powerful king, Portugal's glory declined because of the lack of another strong king.

In 1580, Spain invaded and **annexed** Portugal, making Spain's Phillip II, who was crowned Felipe I, king of Portugal. Under Spain, the country became too weak to hold on to its empire, so it lost much of the land it had held in Asia and Africa. Portugal was able to regain its independence in 1640, but not its former power.

DEMOCRACY TAKES HOLD

As in other European countries, **republicanism** became a widespread idea in Portugal in the 1800s. The recent French Revolution helped to spread the desire for democracy, as did **propaganda** that made its way into Portugal. In 1812, a secret society, the Sinédrio, was formed to pass on revolutionary ideas.

In 1822, a constitutional monarchy was created. While the king still held power, he shared it with a legislative body (the Chamber of Deputies) and a court system. This new constitution created a division in society between those who supported it and those who wanted to go back to a complete monarchy.

Later, another constitution, the Constitutional Charter, was created, giving the king more power. However, in 1828, King Miguel I declared that this constitution was **null**. A later king, Pedro II, restored it. In 1910, the monarchy was completely abolished after many demonstrations and unrest,

Modern-day Portuguese villagers

and a democratic republic was set up in a blood-less revolution.

PROBLEMS WITH DEMOCRACY

For the next fifteen years, Portugal had a troubled and unstable government. The outbreak of World War I did not help the struggling country. In 1916, 40,000 Portuguese forces were sent to fight with the Allies. Unfortunately, they were not well trained or well equipped, and many of the men were killed in the fighting. Learning from its mistakes, Portugal remained neutral in World War II. However, it allowed the Allies to build air and naval bases on Portuguese territory.

Three attempts were made to overthrow the government after democracy was established. One, in 1926, led to dictatorship under António de Oliveira Salazar. His reign was not as oppressive as others of the time, and even included some improvements on society, such as giving women the right to vote. However, people were still unable to freely express their opinions, and all political parties were banned. Salazar's government ended with his death in 1968.

Under Salazar, Portugal's economy grew very slowly. By the middle of the twentieth century, the country was clearly behind those of the rest of Europe and was admitted late to the United Nations, in 1955. After Salazar's death, a success-ful revolt **deposed** his successor, Marcello Caetano, and set up a new, democratic govern-ment.

There was also unrest in many of Portugal's remaining colonies, especially those in Africa.

CHAPTER TWO

Portugal's citizens are now part of the global community.

Portugal lost money dealing with revolts and wars, eventually ending in independence for all of Portugal's colonies in 1974 and 1975.

MODERN PORTUGAL

Over the last few decades, Portugal has slowly recovered some of its lost power and has entered the global community. In 1986, the country joined the European Community, which would eventually become the European Union (EU). It also became a member of the European Monetary Union in 1999.

The current government is much more stable than it has been in the past. The president is elected every five years and can appoint the prime minister. The Council of Ministers makes up the rest of the executive branch. The legislative body is made up the 230-member Assembly of the Republic, a ***unicameral*** house. The government also includes a court system, with the Supreme Court being the highest court. The government has been working hard in recent years to improve the country's rapidly growing economy.

Portugal's beaches draw tourists who contribute to the nation's economy.

3 THE ECONOMY

In the 1800s, Portugal's economy was in trouble, mainly due to political problems. Now, although it is still behind other Western European countries, Portugal has had a relatively stable **capital** economy, allowing it to become one of the founding members of the EU, as well as one of the first eleven countries to adopt the euro, the official currency of the EU. In the past decade, it has even grown at a faster rate than the average

AGRICULTURE

In today's world, most countries have begun to rely less and less on farming to sustain their economies. Portugal's economy, on the other hand, still relies heavily on agriculture. About 14 percent of the population is involved with farming, forestry, or fishing, and slightly more than half of the land on continental Portugal is used for the growing of crops. Most of that land grows olives, wheat, corn, grapes, potatoes, and tomatoes. Fruits, especially citrus fruits like oranges, are also grown.

The products made from these crops are sold throughout the world, as well as locally in Portugal. Portuguese wines and olive oils are especially well known.

A Portuguese shepherd and his flock.

Despite the number of people and land dedicated to agriculture, it provides Portugal with less than 10 percent of its **gross domestic product (GDP)**. This is because not enough modern technology is used to get the most out of agriculture. The solution to this problem is one of Portugal's long-term goals.

GROWING INDUSTRY AND TRADE

Manufacturing and industry have grown in Portugal during the twentieth and twenty-first centuries, especially after it joined the EU. Although it still tends to lag behind other Western European countries, it is slowly establishing itself in industries such as automobile production, electronics, paper manufacturing, and food processing.

Portugal trades mostly with other EU member states. It imports most of its products to EU members such as Spain, Italy, the United Kingdom (UK), Germany, and France. It exports its products to Germany, France, and Spain. Portugal's primary exports are agricultural goods, taking advantage of its supply of cork trees, other wood, and fruit. It imports machinery, cars, oil, and textiles.

Bucaco Palace in the midst of Portugal's forests

NATURAL RESOURCES

One of Portugal's largest resources is wood. Portugal alone provides the world with over half of its supply of cork oak wood. About 34 percent of the land, particularly in the north, is covered in trees, including pine trees, holm oak, cork oak, and eucalyptus.

Mining, although not a major industry, still occurs in Portugal. Tungsten, uranium, and tin are the most abundant minerals that are mined. Coal and copper are also mined.

TRANSPORTATION

Transportation has seen a huge push in growth in recent years. Portugal's highways are modern and extensive, connecting most areas of the country as well as linking it to Spain. The Metro, a type of subway system, can be found in Lisbon and Porto. This public form of transportation is fast and can carry passengers from one part of the city to another fairly inexpensively.

Seaports and airports are also important centers of transportation for the movement of goods and people through and around Portugal. The thousands of miles of coast in the west of Portugal meant that seaports sprung up early. Today, the most important ports are Lisbon, Porto, Setúbal, and Sines. The three major airports on the continent are in Lisbon, Faro, and Porto.

The islands in the Atlantic also have up-to-date transportation. The seaports in Funchal and Ponta Delgada are important links between the Madeira and Azore islands and the rest of the world. Airports in Funchal, Porto Santo, and Ponta Delgada also bring people to and from the islands.

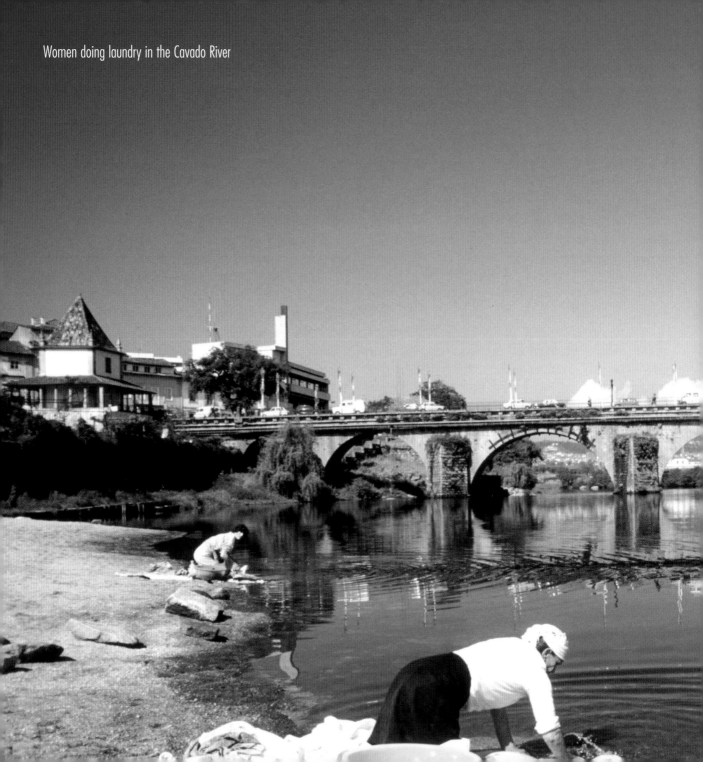

Women doing laundry in the Cavado River

4 Portugal's People and Culture

Portugal tends to have a **homogeneous** population, although the cities are more ethnically diverse. Most Portuguese are descended from the Celt-Iberians; this group mixed with the Romans and Visigoths who later invaded the area. Only about 4 percent of the population today is made up of immigrants, most of whom are Ukrainians, Brazilians, Cape Verdeans, and

Angolans. The lack of diversity means that most Portuguese people have strong ties, socially and historically, to each other; this has created a rich and interesting culture in Portugal.

THE PORTUGUESE LANGUAGE

Spoken by 200 million people, Portuguese is the third most spoken European language in the world, following English and Spanish. This is a visible reminder left by the Portuguese empire in its former colonies, in places like Brazil, Angola, Cape Verde, and East Timor.

In Portugal, the overwhelming majority of people speak Portuguese, which is the official language. Many people have been taught Spanish, English, and French, and can speak them fluently, as in many other European countries.

QUICK FACTS: THE PEOPLE OF PORTUGAL

Population: 10,566,212
Age structure:
  0–14 years: 16.6%
  15–64 years: 66.3%
  65 years and over: 17.1%
Population growth rate: 0.39%
Birth rate: 10.82 births/1,000 population
Death rate: 10.43 deaths/1,000 population
Migration rate: 3.49 migrant(s)/1,000 population
Infant mortality rate: 5.05 deaths/1,000 live births
Life expectancy at birth:
  total population: 77.53 years
  male: 74.25 years
  female: 81.03 years
Total fertility rate: 1.47 children born/woman
Religions: Roman Catholic 94%, Protestant (1995)
Languages: Portuguese (official), Mirandese (not official but locally used)
Literacy: total population: 93.3%

Note: All figures are from 2005 unless otherwise noted.
Source: www.cia.gov, 2005.

RELIGION

Most of Portugal's people are Roman Catholic. Almost 95 percent say they belong to this faith. Protestants make up the largest religious minority, followed by Muslims and Hindus. There is also a tiny number of Jews living in the country.

Despite this lack of religious diversity, Portugal's constitution guarantees its citizens the right to the freedom of religion.

LITERATURE THROUGH THE AGES

Portugal's literature took off during the thirteenth and fourteenth centuries, when troubadours, traveling musicians, and poets spread knowledge throughout the area. In the 1500s, poet Luís

Interior of one of Portugal's many churches

Typical Portuguese fare

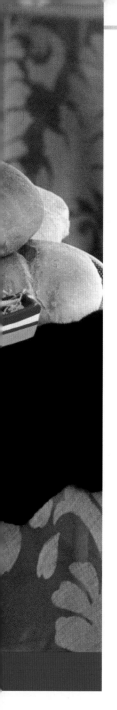

de Camões and **dramatist** Gil Vicente wrote and published several works. De Camões, who wrote the **epic** *The Lusiad*, is celebrated as a national cultural hero today.

Portugal boasts several modern-day writers who have achieved fame. Modern literature includes several poets, including Frenando Pessoa, who wrote during the early 1900s, and writer José Saramago, who won the Nobel Prize for literature in 1998.

THE ARTS: MUSIC AND ARCHITECTURE

Portugal lays claim to the *fado*, a local form of music unique to the country and often described as sad and melancholy. The songs, of which there are thousands, are said to have come from the music of sailors during the sixteenth century, African slave songs, and Arabic music. Folk dancing sometimes accompanies these fados.

Other types of music are popular as well. Hip Hop Tuga, a type of music that is a mix of pop, African music, and reggae, is listened to by the younger generation.

The architecture that can be found in Portugal's cities, as well as its countryside, is often stunning. The Romans, the Moors, and today's **modernism** all influenced the country's buildings. Portugal is also home to one of the best schools for architecture in the world, the Escola do Porto.

SPORTS

As in other European countries, the most popular sport in Portugal is soccer (or football, as it's known in Europe). The Portuguese love to play as much as watch. Portugal has excellent teams, ranked eighth in the world in 2004, and the city of Porto's team has won several world cup titles.

Portugal also has a type of national martial arts, called *Jogo do Pau*, or Portuguese stick combat, since it involves wooden sticks as weapons. The sport originated during medieval times and was used as a style of dueling between young men fighting over a woman. Today, it is a way to celebrate the Portuguese national heritage.

PORTUGUESE CUISINE

The country's close proximity to the sea means that fish and shellfish are a major part of the Portuguese diet. Cod is one of the most widely used fish and is often made into codfish cakes or grilled. Popular foods include grilled sardines (*sardinhas asadas*) and tuna steak (*bife de atúm*).

Child repairing a net

Menus also contain other food grown on Portuguese land, especially potatoes. Perhaps one of the foods most identified with Portugal's cuisine is a custard tart known as a *pastiés de nata*.

Portuguese wines (*vinhos*) are world famous and are enjoyed with meals. Strong coffee is also popular, particularly with dessert.

EDUCATION

Education in Portugal has improved over the past few years, which will hopefully lead to an improvement in the economy when there are more educated workers. Right now, the country has a relatively high **illiteracy rate**.

The current system is divided into *pré-escolar*, which is attended by children younger than six; the *ensino básico*, which children go to for nine years; *ensino secudário*, a three-year level; and *ensino superior*, made up of universities and polytechnic schools. School is free and **compulsory** for nine years, but more and more people are attending higher-level schools.

Education is hoped to bring about changes in jobs, health care, housing, and other social problems. Being a part of the EU also makes these changes real possibilities for the future.

Portugal has resort cities along its coast.

5 CHAPTER THE CITIES

Portugal's cities reflect its long history, as well as the progress the country has made in recent years. A significant portion of the people who live in Portugal are former inhabitants of the colonies Portugal *emancipated* in 1974. Seven percent of the total population is made up of people from places such as the former Portuguese colonies in Africa.

Approximately one-third of the population lives in urban and suburban areas around Lisbon, the capital, and Porto. This reflects the continuing movement of people from rural farming communities to more commercial areas, showing the rising importance of Portugal's cities.

LISBON

Lisbon, or Lisboa in Portuguese, has been Portugal's capital since 1255. As the capital, Lisbon is the center of the government as well as of the culture. The city is home to many cafes, restaurants, and shopping opportunities. It also has over fifty museums; three universities; stunning architecture, such as the Belém and St. George's castle; and historic yellow electric tramcars. The Baixa, or lower town, is an important cultural and historical area of the city.

Its location on the Tagus River gives Lisbon a water trade route, but also a picturesque background. Water sports are popular pastimes, as is strolling along the green banks of the river.

PORTO

Porto is northern Portugal's largest city and the country's second-largest city. The city, which has been made famous by the wine sharing its name, is classified as a UNESCO World Heritage site, demonstrating its importance. Much of the city dates back to medieval times, or even to the period of Roman rule.

In 2001, Porto was declared to be one of the European Culture Capitals. This brought more

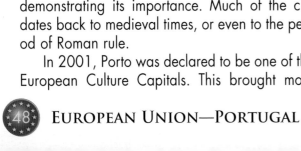

Lisbon's Belem Tower

More and more of Portugal's population are moving to urban areas.

prosperity to the region, as well as a concert hall called Casa da Música. Porto is also home to the Fantasporto International Film Festival.

COIMBRA

Coimbra is another of Portugal's large cities, located between Lisbon and Porto, in the center of Portugal. It is ranked third in importance after these two cities. Like them, Coimbra is a center for culture and history, as well as shopping and dining. Museums, libraries, parks, and monuments attract both locals and tourists.

During the twelfth and thirteenth centuries, Coimbra was Portugal's capital. Today, it is more famous as the home of the University of Coimbra, the seventh-oldest university in Europe. The university contains interesting architecture, as does the rest of the city. Because the city is so old, Roman ruins can be found at the city's archeological site.

LAGOS

Located on the coast of the Algarve, Lagos attracts many tourists. The beaches are breathtaking, and the weather is consistently warm. Tourists and locals alike can enjoy the sun and the outdoors by renting mopeds or taking boat trips from the harbor. Culturally, Lagos is known for the Museu Municipal, a fascinating museum that contains unusual exhibits.

The EU flag

6

THE FORMATION OF THE EUROPEAN UNION

The EU is an economic and political confederation of twenty-five European nations. Member countries abide by common foreign and security policies and cooperate on judicial and domestic affairs. The confederation, however, does not replace existing states or governments. Each of the twenty-five member states is **autonomous**, but they have all agreed to establish some common institutions and to hand over some of their own decision-making powers to these international bodies. As a result, decisions on matters that interest all member states can be made democratically, accommodating everyone's concerns and interests.

Today, the EU is the most powerful regional organization in the world. It has evolved from a primarily economic organization to an increasingly political one. Besides promoting economic cooperation, the EU requires that its members uphold fundamental values of peace and **solidarity**, human dignity, freedom, and equality. Based on the principles of democracy and the rule of law, the EU respects the culture and organizations of member states.

HISTORY

The seeds of the EU were planted more than fifty years ago in a Europe reduced to smoking piles of rubble by two world wars. European nations suffered great financial difficulties in the postwar period. They were struggling to get back on their feet and realized that another war would cause further hardship. Knowing that internal conflict was hurting all of Europe, a drive began toward European cooperation.

France took the first historic step. On May 9, 1950 (now celebrated as Europe Day), Robert Schuman, the French foreign minister, proposed the coal and steel industries of France and West Germany be coordinated under a single supranational authority. The proposal, known as the Treaty of Paris, attracted four other countries—Belgium, Luxembourg, the Netherlands, and Italy—and resulted in the 1951 formation of the European Coal and Steel Community (ECSC). These six countries became the founding members of the EU.

In 1957, European cooperation took its next big leap. Under the Treaty of Rome, the European Economic Community (EEC) and the European Atomic Energy Community (EURATOM) were formed. Informally known as the Common Market, the EEC promoted joining the national economies into a single European economy. The 1965 Treaty of Brussels (more commonly referred to as the Merger Treaty) united these various treaty organizations under a single umbrella, the European Community (EC).

In 1992, the Maastricht Treaty (also known as the Treaty of the European Union) was signed in Maastricht, the Netherlands, signaling the birth of the EU as it stands today. **Ratified** the following year, the Maastricht Treaty provided for a central banking system, a common currency (the euro) to replace the national currencies, a legal definition of the EU, and a framework for expanding the

The EU's united economy has allowed it to become a worldwide financial power.

EU's political role, particularly in the area of foreign and security policy.

By 1993, the member countries completed their move toward a single market and agreed to participate in a larger common market, the European Economic Area, established in 1994.

The EU, headquartered in Brussels, Belgium, reached its current member strength in spurts. In

© BCE ECB EZB EKT EKP 2002

© BCE ECB EZB EKT EKP 2002

© BCE ECB EZB EKT EKP 2002

© BCE ECB EZB EKT EKP 2002

The euro, the EU's currency

1973, Denmark, Ireland, and the United Kingdom joined the six founding members of the EC. They were followed by Greece in 1981, and Portugal and Spain in 1986. The 1990s saw the unification of the two Germanys, and as a result, East Germany entered the EU fold. Austria, Finland, and Sweden joined the EU in 1995, bringing the total number of member states to fifteen. In 2004, the EU nearly doubled its size when ten countries—Cyprus, the Czech Republic, Estonia, Hungary, Latvia, Lithuania, Malta, Poland, Slovakia, and Slovenia—became members.

THE EU FRAMEWORK

The EU's structure has often been compared to a "roof of a temple with three columns." As established by the Maastricht Treaty, this three-pillar framework encompasses all the policy areas—or pillars—of European cooperation. The three pillars of the EU are the European Community, the Common Foreign and Security Policy (CFSP), and Police and Judicial Co-operation in Criminal Matters.

QUICK FACTS: THE EUROPEAN UNION

Number of Member Countries: 25

Official Languages: 20—Czech, Danish, Dutch, English, Estonian, Finnish, French, German, Greek, Hungarian, Italian, Latvian, Lithuanian, Maltese, Polish, Portuguese, Slovak, Slovenian, Spanish, and Swedish; additional language for treaty purposes: Irish Gaelic

Motto: *In Varietate Concordia* (United in Diversity)

European Council's President: Each member state takes a turn to lead the council's activities for 6 months.

European Commission's President: José Manuel Barroso (Portugal)

European Parliament's President: Josep Borrell (Spain)

Total Area: 1,502,966 square miles (3,892,685 sq. km.)

Population: 454,900,000

Population Density: 302.7 people/square mile (116.8 people/sq. km.)

GDP: €9.61.1012

Per Capita GDP: €21,125

Formation:
- Declared: February 7, 1992, with signing of the Maastricht Treaty
- Recognized: November 1, 1993, with the ratification of the Maastricht Treaty

Community Currency: Euro. Currently 12 of the 25 member states have adopted the euro as their currency.

Anthem: "Ode to Joy"

Flag: Blue background with 12 gold stars arranged in a circle

Official Day: Europe Day, May 9

Source: europa.eu.int

PILLAR ONE

The European Community pillar deals with economic, social, and environmental policies. It is a body consisting of the European Parliament, European Commission, European Court of Justice, Council of the European Union, and the European Courts of Auditors.

PILLAR TWO

The idea that the EU should speak with one voice in world affairs is as old as the European integration process itself. Toward this end, the Common Foreign and Security Policy (CFSP) was formed in 1993.

Pillar Three

The cooperation of EU member states in judicial and criminal matters ensures that its citizens enjoy the freedom to travel, work, and live securely and safely anywhere within the EU. The third pillar—Police and Judicial Co-operation in Criminal Matters—helps to protect EU citizens from international crime and to ensure equal access to justice and fundamental rights across the EU.

The flags of the EU's nations:

top row, left to right
Belgium, the Czech Republic, Denmark, Germany, Estonia, Greece

second row, left to right
Spain, France, Ireland, Italy, Cyprus, Latvia

third row, left to right
Lithuania, Luxembourg, Hungary, Malta, the Netherlands, Austria

bottom row, left to right
Poland, Portugal, Slovenia, Slovakia, Finland, Sweden, United Kingdom

Economic Status

As of May 2004, the EU had the largest economy in the world, followed closely by the United States. But even though the EU continues to enjoy a trade surplus, it faces the twin problems of high unemployment rates and ***stagnancy***.

The 2004 addition of ten new member states is expected to boost economic growth. EU membership is likely to stimulate the economies of these relatively poor countries. In turn, their prosperity growth will be beneficial to the EU.

The Euro

The EU's official currency is the euro, which came into circulation on January 1, 2002. The shift to the euro has been the largest monetary changeover in the world. Twelve countries—Belgium, Germany, Greece, Spain, France, Ireland, Italy, Luxembourg, the Netherlands, Finland, Portugal, and Austria—have adopted it as their currency.

Single Market

Within the EU, laws of member states are harmonized and domestic policies are coordinated to create a larger, more-efficient single market.

The chief features of the EU's internal policy on the single market are:

- free trade of goods and services

- a common EU competition law that controls anticompetitive activities of companies and member states

- removal of internal border control and harmonization of external controls between member states

- freedom for citizens to live and work anywhere in the EU as long as they are not dependent on the state

- free movement of capital between member states

- harmonization of government regulations, corporation law, and trademark registration

- a single currency

- coordination of environmental policy

- a common agricultural policy and a common fisheries policy

- a common system of indirect taxation, the value-added tax (VAT), and common customs duties and **excise**

- funding for research

- funding for aid to disadvantaged regions

The EU's external policy on the single market specifies:

- a common external **tariff** and a common position in international trade negotiations

- funding of programs in other Eastern European countries and developing countries

COOPERATION AREAS

EU member states cooperate in other areas as well. Member states can vote in European Parliament elections. Intelligence sharing and cooperation in criminal matters are carried out through EUROPOL and the Schengen Information System.

The EU is working to develop common foreign and security policies. Many member states are resisting such a move, however, saying these are sensitive areas best left to individual member states. Arguing in favor of a common approach to security and foreign policy are countries like France and Germany, who insist that a safer and more secure Europe can only become a reality under the EU umbrella.

One of the EU's great achievements has been to create a boundary-free area within which people, goods, services, and money can move around freely; this ease of movement is sometimes called "the four freedoms." As the EU grows in size, so do the challenges facing it—and yet its fifty-year history has amply demonstrated the power of cooperation.

Europe is proud of its "bright idea," a union with economic and political power.

The EU believes that it can use its power to act as a "lighthouse" for the rest of the world.

KEY EU INSTITUTIONS

Five key institutions play a specific role in the EU.

THE EUROPEAN PARLIAMENT

The European Parliament (EP) is the democratic voice of the people of Europe. Directly elected every five years, the Members of the European Parliament (MEPs) sit not in national **blocs** but in political groups representing the seven main political parties of the member states. Each group reflects the political ideology of the national parties to which its members belong. Some MEPs are not attached to any political group.

COUNCIL OF THE EUROPEAN UNION

The Council of the European Union (formerly known as the Council of Ministers) is the main leg-

islative and decision-making body in the EU. It brings together the nationally elected representatives of the member-state governments. One minister from each of the EU's member states attends council meetings. It is the forum in which government representatives can assert their interests and reach compromises. Increasingly, the Council of the European Union and the EP are acting together as colegislators in decision-making processes.

EUROPEAN COMMISSION

The European Commission does much of the day-to-day work of the EU. Politically independent, the commission represents the interests of the EU as a whole, rather than those of individual member states. It drafts proposals for new European laws, which it presents to the EP and the Council of the European Union. The European Commission makes sure EU decisions are implemented properly and supervises the way EU funds are spent. It also sees that everyone abides by the European treaties and European law.

The EU member-state governments choose the European Commission president, who is then approved by the EP. Member states, in consultation with the incoming president, nominate the other European Commission members, who must also be approved by the EP. The commission is appointed for a five-year term, but can be dismissed by the EP. Many members of its staff work in Brussels, Belgium.

COURT OF JUSTICE

Headquartered in Luxembourg, the Court of Justice of the European Communities consists of one independent judge from each EU country. This court ensures that the common rules decided in the EU are understood and followed uniformly by all the members. The Court of Justice settles disputes over how EU treaties and legislation are interpreted. If national courts are in doubt about how to apply EU rules, they must ask the Court of Justice. Individuals can also bring proceedings against EU institutions before the court.

COURT OF AUDITORS

EU funds must be used legally, economically, and for their intended purpose. The Court of Auditors, an independent EU institution located in Luxembourg, is responsible for overseeing how EU money is spent. In effect, these auditors help European taxpayers get better value for the money that has been channeled into the EU.

OTHER IMPORTANT BODIES

1. European Economic and Social Committee: expresses the opinions of organized civil society on economic and social issues

2. Committee of the Regions: expresses the opinions of regional and local authorities

3. European Central Bank: responsible for monetary policy and managing the euro

4. European Ombudsman: deals with citizens' complaints about mismanagement by any EU institution or body

5. European Investment Bank: helps achieve EU objectives by financing investment projects

Together with a number of agencies and other bodies completing the system, the EU's institutions have made it the most powerful organization in the world.

EU MEMBER STATES

In order to become a member of the EU, a country must have a stable democracy that guarantees the rule of law, human rights, and protection of minorities. It must also have a functioning market economy as well as a civil service capable of applying and managing EU laws.

The EU provides substantial financial assistance and advice to help candidate countries prepare themselves for membership. As of October 2004, the EU has twenty-five member states. Bulgaria and Romania are likely to join in 2007, which would bring the EU's total population to nearly 500 million.

In December 2004, the EU decided to open negotiations with Turkey on its proposed membership. Turkey's possible entry into the EU has been fraught with controversy. Much of this controversy has centered on Turkey's human rights record and the divided island of Cyprus. If allowed to join the EU, Turkey would be its most-populous member state.

The 2004 expansion was the EU's most ambitious enlargement to date. Never before has the EU embraced so many new countries, grown so much in terms of area and population, or encompassed so many different histories and cultures. As the EU moves forward into the twenty-first century, it will undoubtedly continue to grow in both political and economic strength.

Stormy waters off Portugal's coast

7 PORTUGAL IN THE EUROPEAN UNION

Portugal is one of the oldest members of the EU. It joined the organization along with Spain. Together, the two nations brought to the EU a new, Iberian perspective on European affairs and prob-

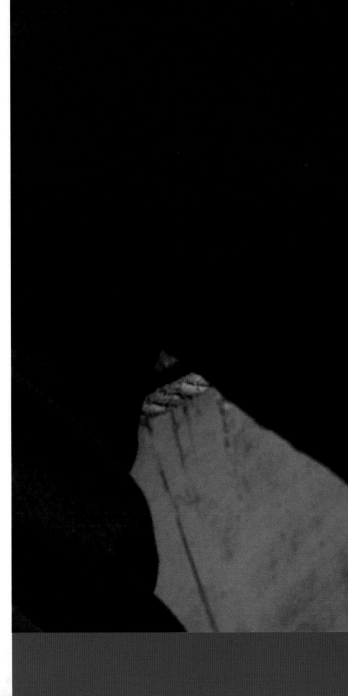

A Fledgling Relationship

Portugal originally joined the EU, then known as the European Economic Community (EEC) in 1986. Although both Portugal and Spain were welcomed into the EU, several member countries became worried, including the UK, France, and Germany. They began to consider the possibility that with the **induction** of new, poorer countries, the original nations would have to deal with waves of immigrants. People who wanted to get away from the poverty and misfortune they experienced in places like Portugal and Spain might take advantage of the open borders created by accession to the EU.

This fear died down after the two countries joined, and the masses of poor immigrants failed to appear. However, this same worry cropped up again when the EU considered the accession of eleven new members in 2004. Most of these potential members were poverty-stricken Eastern European nations.

Help from the EU

With EU membership, Portugal was given financial aid that was meant to help its economy grow and to ease social problems. Portugal needed that money to meet the standards the EU set for membership.

Portugal used the EU aid to improve its **infrastructure**. Money went to things like roads, communications, hospitals, and schools. Thanks to this assistance, Portugal was slowly

Knitting nets the traditional way

Rock formations at Praia da Rocha in Algarve

able to achieve a much more stable economy that continued to grow. As a result, Portugal now does not need as much economic assistance. In fact, Lisbon has improved so much that the EU is planning to stop providing the area with aid.

Money was not the only thing that EU membership brought to Portugal. Trade also played an important factor in the country's growth. Trade with fellow member states became much easier with increased access to markets for the goods produced in Portugal. Today, Portugal continues to conduct most of its trade with other members of the EU.

PORTUGAL'S POSITION IN THE EU

A major debate has been going on within the EU concerning the direction that EU policies should take during the twenty-first century. The debate is between those countries that favor intergovernmentalism and those that support supranationalism.

Supporters of intergovernmentalism believe that the EU's decisions should be made unanimously. Countries such as the United Kingdom, Sweden, and Denmark favor this approach because they want to maintain their freedom to govern themselves to at least a limited extent, while still having a say in the EU's affairs. Under a supranationalist approach, decisions are made by majority votes of elected officials or representatives. Those who support this type of government believe it would take too long to make decisions based on unanimity. France, Germany, and Italy support this type of EU.

One of Portugal's many waterfront villages

Portugal and its people tend to favor supranationalism. In a poll conducted in 2004, 60 percent of the Portuguese people trusted the EU. Portugal supports the closer **integration** of European countries and sees the benefits to working in a close-knit community.

PORTUGAL'S ROLE TODAY AND TOMORROW

In 1986, Portugal was a newly inducted and powerless nation—but it has come a long way since then. Today, Portugal has become one of the leading powers of the EU. The country has held the presidency of the EU twice, most recently in the first half of 2000. During this presidency, it worked to strengthen ties between the EU and Africa and tried to improve the economy of the EU as a whole.

Today, Portugal is a fully functioning member of the EU. It has twenty-four seats in the EU Parliament and twelve votes in the Council. Portugal also contributes nearly 1.5 billion euros to the EU's budget.

From its rich history, to its fascinating cities, to its interesting people, Portugal is poised to help bring peace and prosperity to the EU, as well as to itself. Its future looks hopeful for both its people and its economy as it begins to work more closely with its neighboring European countries.

A Calendar of Portugese Festivals

January: Many northern Portuguese families observe **Epiphany** on January 6 by eating Bolo-Rei (King Cake) and singing traditional songs.

February: Carnaval, celebrated the day before **Ash Wednesday**, often falls in February, six weeks before Easter. Carnaval is one of the biggest holidays in Portugal and is marked by parties and parades. Originally a pagan festival, it now has ties to Christianity.

March/April: Easter, or Páscoa as it's known in Portugal, is a religious, as well as family, holiday. Families eat Easter cake and decorate Easter eggs while church members bless homes. Picnics are often eaten on the Monday after Easter, known as **Dia do Anjo**, or Angel Day. **Dia de Liberdade** is celebrated on April 25 to remember the end of Portugal's dictatorship in 1974.

June: During this month, three saints, known as the Santos Populares, are celebrated. Saint Anthony is celebrated with **Marchas Populares**, or carnivals, on June 12 and 13. On June 23 and 24, people often hammer on each other's heads with plastic hammers to celebrate Saint John. Saint Peter is usually remembered with fires on June 28 and 29. June 10, **Dia de Portugal**, or Portugal Day, marks the death date of the writer of *The Lusiad*, a national epic.

October: Republic Day is observed June 5 in commemoration of the establishment of the Republic in 1910.

November: All Saints Day, on November 1, is a day for remembering loved ones who have died. On November 11, people celebrate **Saint Martin Day** with roasted chestnuts and drinks.

December: Portugal's **Independence Day** is on December 1, commemorating independence from Spain in 1640. Christmas, or **Natal**, on December 24 and 25 is celebrated with family gatherings where food such as codfish, sweets, and dried fruits are eaten, and gifts are given.

Sweet Bread
(Broa Doce)

Makes one 9-inch round loaf

Ingredients
1/4 cup butter or margarine, melted
3/4 cup 1% milk
1/3 cup granulated sugar
1 packet active dry yeast
2 eggs, room temperature
3–3 1/4 cups flour
1/2 teaspoon salt
1 egg yolk
2 tablespoons water
1 tablespoon coarse or raw sugar

Directions
Melt butter in saucepan on stovetop. Add milk and sugar; stir well and heat to 110°F, slightly more than lukewarm. Pour into mixing bowl, stir in yeast to dissolve and let stand 10 minutes. Beat in eggs, then gradually beat in flour mixed with salt. On a lightly floured surface, knead dough until smooth and elastic. Cover with a damp towel and let rise until doubled.

Punch dough down, shape into a 7-inch round. Place in greased 9-inch cake pan. Beat egg yolk with water and brush over dough; sprinkle with sugar. Cover with damp towel and let rise in a warm place until doubled.

Preheat oven to 350°F. Bake 45 to 50 minutes, or until well browned and hollow sounding when tapped lightly. Cool on rack. Serve warm or toasted. To serve, cut bread into quarters, then slice each quarter into five slices, each about 1 inch thick.

Classic Portuguese Beans
(Feijao a Portuguesa)

6 to 8 servings

Ingredients
1 pound dried navy, great northern or other small white beans
Water as needed
1/2 pound bacon
1 large onion, chopped
3 garlic cloves, minced
1 6-ounce can tomato paste
1 pound Spanish (not Mexican) chorizo, or other spicy smoked sausage, cut into 1/4-inch slices
1/2 teaspoon dried red pepper flakes
1 tablespoon sweet paprika
Salt and freshly ground pepper to taste

Directions
Wash beans. Soak beans overnight in enough cold water to cover by several inches. Before using the next day, drain and rinse beans and set aside.

Fry bacon in skillet over medium heat until crisp, 5 minutes. Drain on paper towels and set aside.

Pour off all but 2 or 3 tablespoons of bacon fat, add onion and cook until golden brown, 8 to 10 minutes. Add garlic and cook 1 minute more. Add beans, 8 cups water, tomato paste, chorizo, red pepper flakes, and paprika. Cover and simmer until beans are tender, 1 1/2 to 2 hours, stirring occasionally to prevent scorching.

Just before serving, crumble bacon into beans and season with salt and pepper.

Comments: Depending on the size and age of the beans you use, the cooking time could vary considerably. If the beans threaten to dry out, add water; if they're watery, remove the cover for the last half hour of cooking. Spanish chorizo is available at Spanish and some Latin markets.

Cream Custards
(Pasteis De Nata)

This recipe yields 12 servings.

Ingredients
Pastry:
2 cup flour plus more
1 teaspoon salt
2 tablespoons sugar
10 tablespoons chilled butter cut into 1/4-inch cubes
5–7 tablespoons ice water

Custard:
1 tablespoon cornstarch
1 1/2 cups whipping cream
1 cup sugar
6 egg yolks

Directions
For the pastry: In bowl or food processor fitted with metal blade, pulse flour, salt, and sugar to combine. Add butter and pulse until flour resembles coarse, uneven cornmeal, about 10 one-second pulses. Drizzle 5 tablespoons ice water over mixture. Pulse several times to work water into flour. If the mixture is too dry, add the remaining water, 1 tablespoon at a time, and continue pulsing until mixture develops small curds. Turn dough out onto work surface, shape into a disc, and cover in plastic wrap. Refrigerate at least 1 hour.

On lightly floured surface, roll half the dough to 1/16-inch thickness. Cut out 6 (4 1/2-inch) circles. Ease dough circles into a 12-cup (4-ounce capacity) nonstick muffin pan, pressing out any overlap. Repeat with remaining dough. Place in freezer 5 minutes. Trim overhang with knife. Line dough cups with cupcake papers and fill with dried beans or pastry weights. Bake at 350°F for 8 to 10 minutes. Set aside to cool.

For the custard: Dissolve cornstarch in 1/4-cup whipping cream in medium bowl. Add remaining cream and sugar, and stir until mixture is smooth and sugar dissolves. (To see if the sugar has dissolved, insert a spoon. When removed, there should be no sugar sticking to it.) In a small bowl, blend yolks with fork until smooth. Add to cream mixture, stirring gently to combine.

Ladle egg mixture into pastry cups, filling to 2/3 capacity. Bake at 350°F until edges of custard are puffed but the middle is still jiggly, 20 to 25 minutes. (Custard will continue to cook after removing from oven.) Cool completely in pan. Best when eaten the same day.

Eggs Portuguese-Style

Ingredients
1 tablespoon olive oil
1 medium onion, chopped
1/2 green bell pepper, chopped
1 clove garlic, minced
1 pound zucchini, diced
1/2 cup tomato sauce
1 tablespoon minced parsley
1/2 teaspoon dried basil
1/2 teaspoon dried oregano
3 large eggs
1/4 cup skim milk
1/4 teaspoon salt
1/8 teaspoon pepper
1/2 cup (2 ounces) shredded mild cheddar cheese

Directions
Heat oil in a wide, broiler-proof frying pan over medium-high heat. Add onion, bell pepper, garlic, and zucchini. Cook, stirring occasionally, for 5 minutes. Reduce heat to medium-low, cover and cook 5 more minutes, or until zucchini is crisp and tender. Add tomato sauce, parsley, basil, and oregano. Simmer, uncovered, about 5 minutes, until sauce thickens slightly.

In a bowl, combine eggs, milk, salt, and pepper; whisk until evenly blended. Pour over zucchini mixture. Cover frying pan and cook 5 minutes, or until eggs are set but still moist on top. Sprinkle cheese over eggs.

Preheat broiler. Place frying pan 6 inches under broiler. Broil 1 minute or until cheese melts. Cut into wedges and serve from pan.

PROJECT AND REPORT IDEAS

Maps

- Make a map of the eurozone, and create a legend to indicate key manufacturing industries throughout the EU.
- Create an export map of Portugal using a legend to represent all the major products exported by Portugal. The map should clearly indicate all of Portugal's industrial and agricultural regions.

Reports

- Write a brief report on Portugal's growing industries.
- Write a report on Portugal's concerns within the EU.
- Write a brief report on any of the following historical events: the Reconquest, the Carnation Revolution, Portugal's accession into the EU.
- Portugal set up colonies in many parts of the world. Research and write a report on where these colonies were and how those countries were affected by Portugal.

Biographies
Write a one-page biography on one of the following:

- Prince Henry the Navigator
- António de Oliveira Salazar
- Lúis de Camões

Journals

- Imagine that you are a Jew living in Portugal during the Portuguese Inquisition. Write a journal that describes the decision you and your family must make whether to flee the country or face persecution. Include the reasons behind your choice.
- In the eleventh century, the Moors were driven out of Portugal by Christians during the Reconquest. Write a journal from the point of view of a Moor, describing how you feel about the Reconquest.

Projects

- Learn the Portuguese expressions for simple words such as hello, good day, please, thank you. Try them on your friends.
- Make a calendar of your country's festivals and list the ones that are common or similar in Portugal. Are they celebrated differently in Portugal? If so, how?
- Go online or to the library and find images of Moorish Portuguese architecture. Make a model of one example.
- Make a list of all the rivers, places, seas, and islands that you have read about in this book and indicate them on a map of Portugal.
- Find a Portuguese recipe other than the ones given in this book, and ask an adult to help you make it. Share it with members of your class.

Group Activities

- Debate: One side should take the role of Portugal and the other Britain. Portugal's position is that the EU should adopt a supranational approach, while Britain will speak in favor of the intergovernmental mode.
- Role play: Reenact a scene in which Portugal has given one of its colonies freedom.

CHRONOLOGY

5500 BCE	Fortified villages are established in Tagus Valley.
700 BCE	Celts arrive on Iberian Peninsula.
219 BCE	Romans invade the Iberian Peninsula.
c.400 CE	Visigoths take over Iberia.
711 CE	Moors invade Portugal, and the Golden Age begins.
c.1000	Moors are driven out of peninsula by Christians; Christian Reconquest of the peninsula begins.
1143	Portugal is officially recognized as a country.
1400s	Portugal enters age of expansion.
1539	Court of Inquisition set up.
1580	Spain annexes Portugal.
1640	Portugal regains its independence from Spain.
1812	Sinédrio is set up to spread revolutionary ideas.
1822	Constitutional monarchy created.
1828	King Miguel I declares the constitution null.
1910	The monarchy is abolished and a democratic republic is established.
1916	Portugal enters World War I.
1926	The military takes over the government, and Salazar becomes dictator.
1955	Portugal is admitted to the United Nations.
1968	Salazar dies.
1974	Caetano is overthrown, and a new democracy is formed; Portuguese colonies are given their independence.
1986	Portugal becomes a founding member of the EU.

FURTHER READING/INTERNET RESOURCES

Blauer, Ettagale, and Jason Laure. *Portugal.* New York: Scholastic Library Publishing, 2001.
Heale, Jay. *Portugal.* New York: Benchmark Books, 1995.
Hole, Abigail, and Charlotte Beech. *Portugal,* 5th ed. Footscray, Victoria, Australia, 2005.
Luard, Elisabeth. *The Food of Spain and Portugal: A Regional Celebration.* London: Kyle Books, 2005.
Saramago, José. *Journey to Portugal: In Pursuit of Portugal's History and Culture.* New York: Harcourt, 2001.

Travel Information
www.portugal.org/tourism/info/shtml
www.portugaltravelguide.com

History and Geography
lcweb2.loc.gov/frd/cs/pttoc.html
worldfacts.us/Portugal-geography.htm
www.historyofnations.net/europe/portugal.html

Culture and Festivals
www.2camels.com/festivals/festivals_in_portugal.php3
www.portcult.com

Economic and Political Information
encyclopedia.laborlawtalk.com/Politics_of_Portugal
www.nationmaster.com/country/po/Economy

EU Information
europa.eu.int/

FOR MORE INFORMATION

Embassy of Portugal
2125 Kalorama Rd., NW
Washington, DC 20008
Tel.: 202-328-8610

Permanent Mission of Portugal to the United Nations
866 Second Avenue, 9th Floor
New York, NY 10017
Tel.: 212-759-9444

U.S. Department of State
2201 C Street NW
Washington, DC 20520
Tel.: 202-647-4000

U.S. Embassy
Avenida das Forças Armadas
1600-081 Lisbon, Portugal
Tel.: 351-21-727-3300

GLOSSARY

annexed: Took over territory and incorporated it into another political entity.

archipelagoes: Groups or chains of islands.

assimilated: Integrated into a larger group in such a manner that differences are minimized or eliminated.

autonomous: Able to act independently.

blocs: United groups of countries.

capital: Wealth in the form of money or property.

compulsory: Required.

deforestation: The act of removing trees from an area.

deposed: Removed someone from office or from a position of power.

dramatist: Someone who writes plays.

emancipated: Freed.

epic: A long narrative.

excise: A government-imposed tax on goods used domestically.

gross domestic product (GDP): The total value of goods and services produced in a country in one year.

hereditary: Passed down, or capable of being passed down, from generation to generation.

heresy: An opinion contrary to church teaching.

homogeneous: Having the same structure or characteristics throughout.

hunter-gatherers: Members of a society whose food is obtained through hunting, fishing, and foraging only.

illiteracy rate: The percentage of a country's population who cannot read and write.

induction: The act of admitting someone to an organization.

infrastructure: A country's large-scale public works, such as utilities and roads, necessary for economic activity.

integration: Opening an organization to everyone.

modernism: The latest styles, tastes, and trends.

null: Having no legal validity.

propaganda: Information or publicity given by a government or organization in support of a doctrine or cause.

ratified: Officially approved.

republicanism: A belief that a country's power should rest with its voters.

solidarity: Presenting a united front.

stagnancy: A period of inactivity.

tariff: A government-imposed tax on imported goods.

temperate: Not extreme.

unanimously: Done with complete agreement.

unicameral: Having one house of government.

INDEX

agriculture 34–35
ancient Portugal 20
architecture 43

Celts 20
climate 14
coasts and rivers 13

Coimbra 51

dating systems 20

economy 33–37
education 45
environmental concerns 17
European Union (EU) 31, 52–73
    cooperation areas 60
    economic status 59
    euro 59
    framework 57–59
    history 54–55, 57
    key institutions 62–63, 65
    member states 65
    Portugal in 67–73
    single market 59–60

flora and fauna 14, 17
food and drink 43, 45

geography 12–13, 14

industry and trade 35
the Inquisition 24
the islands 13

Lagos 51
language 40
Lisbon 12, 48
literature 40, 43

modern Portugal 31
the Moors 20, 23
music 43

natural resources 37

Porto 48, 51

religion 40
Romans 20, 21

sports 43

transportation 37

PICTURE CREDITS

BIOGRAPHIES

AUTHOR

Kim Etingoff currently lives in Vestal, New York, where she has lived for most of her life. She contributes to a small local newspaper, where she holds the position of editor in chief. A recent trip to Europe helped to foster her interest in other countries, cultures, and peoples.

SERIES CONSULTANTS

Ambassador John Bruton served as Irish Prime Minister from 1994 until 1997. As prime minister, he helped turn Ireland's economy into one of the fastest-growing in the world. He was also involved in the Northern Ireland Peace Process, which led to the 1998 Good Friday Agreement. During his tenure as Ireland's prime minister, he also presided over the European Union presidency in 1996 and helped finalize the Stability and Growth Pact, which governs management of the euro. Before being named the European Commission Head of Delegation in the United States, he was a member of the convention that drafted the European Constitution, signed October 29, 2004.

The European Commission Delegation to the United States represents the interests of the European Union as a whole, much as ambassadors represent their countries' interests to the U.S. government. Matters coming under European Commission authority are negotiated between the commission and the U.S. administration.